Naked

vol. 1

Charlie Puffer

Fuel your life with inspiration.

~ Charlie

SOURCE

I write from
a place of pain
a place of hope
a place of love
the end of a rope.

I write from
a place of longing
and grief.
I write for the false sense
of relief.

I write from desperation
a plea to my nation,
the people in my community
trying to establish immunity
from the crimes of our
corporately branded
fascist federation.

I write because
it's what I can do
whether you like it or not.
I write because
aside from pouring drinks
and telling blue jokes
it's all I've got.

I write because
I am not a musician.
If I was I would sing
and sing and moan and wail
I would play my axe
until my body failed
to uphold the hollow bodied
vessel of life.

I write because I can't not.

I write because I'm not
Mahatma Ghandi
Mohammed Ali
Mother Theresa
Nelson Mandela
Martin Luther King Jr
Abraham Lincoln
to name a few.
I write 'cause I've got
nothing better to do.

I write because I'm not
Superman
Batman
Spiderman
Hell, I'm not even Green Lantern.

I write because
I want to embrace all.
Even the assholes
that are ruining our world.

I write because
if I didn't
I might explode,
and I don't want to foot
the dry cleaning bill
to get the Puff stains
out of your garments.

Thank you for listening.

WATER, BABY

The encompassing aura
of the crashing waves
one of nature's symphonies
backed by the winds
buttressed by tides
the ocean's liquid tympani.

The constant thrumming
of water on land
hints that maybe
there is a God's hand
manipulating
the coastal sand
I hope she's not got
it in for me.

I have spent many nights
exposed to the world
on mountains
in deserts
the plains
the coast
the manic big cities
that tax you the most.
The ocean, however,
is your eternal host.

Unforgiving
unrepentant
the ocean cares not
for our insignificance;
it just wields its power
it rages, it swells
sometimes placid
continuing in its
omnipotent dance.

I have spent much time
in the oceans of life
sometimes naked
sometimes on a boat;
I've realized that
the valuable thing
is the ability to float.

STATE OF MIND

I am not fiercely sober
like my worthy friend,
but passionately drinking
constantly thinking
not sinking
into a maudlin end.

I feel this world's
gravity
requires not depravity
but positivity
pervasive levity
an underlying funk.
That's why I spend
a lot of time drunk.

You won't find me
cruising the avenues.
I'll be massaging
my keyboard
seeking my muse
singing my blues
igniting my fuse
paying my dues
refusing
the obtuse screws
of those who abuse
the better natures
of the few,
ignoring the clues.

Those elixirs,
temporal fixers
of wounded humanity

give respite
to the overly conscious minds
of those seeking sanity.

Here
it may appear
that I gloat
while floating
in the wake of a boat
of cocktails and toasts
flowing towards
an unknown fate.
In reality
I'm just punching back
at the agents of hate.

This may seem
a passive choice
but the brio of booze
gives me a voice
to counteract the noise
these hungry power boys
hiss and spit
in the name of a savior;
I prefer my own behavior.

We can't all get along.
We never will.
We can be patient.
We can be still.
Reserving judgment
until such time
as action is needed
at which point
we'll take that hill.

GHOST WALTZ

Rolled out this morning
just shy of five
grateful as a schoolboy
to still be alive.

Bottle on the counter
pour myself a shot
choke down the poison
back to my cot.

Cold arms embrace me
affection from the grave
my feeble heart betrays me
there is no soul to save.

I roll back into coma
sleep is no relief
in darkness I work overtime
examining my grief

for all of those
I've loved and lost
all that I have wasted
all that I have consumed
the bitter, sweet I've tasted.

Adios, amigos
I owe so much to you
I wish you peace and happiness
in all that you may do.

In this life
and whatever is next,
that which was not planned,
in the fury of your freefall
lash out and grasp my hand.

Not sure if I'm holding you
or you are holding me
but hold on tight, don't let go
we've got more things to be.

MIDNIGHT FLIGHT

Beneath the midnight stars
in Pismo Beach
my dreams seem
not so far from reach;

A fog encroaches
shroud of mystery —
Some unknown fate
pursuing me?

Soon the vapor dissipates
latent anxiety abates;
The stars return,
the silver sliver moon,
perhaps I'll return
to slumber soon.

Some lucky souls
sleep through the night,
not I
engaged in nocturnal fight
between what is wrong or right

a grand canyon,
fissure of dreams
versus reality,
what I have wrought of my life,
was it meant to be?

"Nothing is written!"
Lawrence said;
tomorrow's labor is written
now back to bed.

AIR TRAFFIC CONTROL

The birds swoop by,
little flapping missiles
in the sky.
Not delivering
destruction
but the construction
of their own bird realities.

I observe them
enviously,
wishing that I could be
airborn
and apparently
carefree.

We all have
our own wings
and flight patterns,
yet grounded by our
need for things,
things,
always more things.

We are
Earthbound
by gravity
but the pervasive
depravity of need
for things, more things
clips our wings.

I understand
the nature
of our beastliness,

but I would feast
on less
in the pursuit of
more time unhinged
by the limitations
that impinge on us.

We may soar
in the absence
of our inhibitions
with the proper
omission
of the forces
that belittle us.

In the middle of the night
we might,
if we free ourselves
just right,
take flight.

We feel the weight
of obligation
the consummation
of our programming
and expectations.

Let us free ourselves
to be ourselves
and soar, baby, soar
into whatever
blue horizons
await.

MISTAKEN IDENTITY

She thought she knew me
but she couldn't.
She thought she'd do me,
but she wouldn't.
She tried to impress on me
things she shouldn't.

Now I'm naked alone
in the middle of the day
wondering how
things got this way.

Bare to the planet,
nude to the brood,
vulnerable,
another foolish dude.

It's not a contest,
it's not a game;
it's not about guilt,
it's not about shame.

It's about discovery
of one's self
and of others;
do not wear the armor
that is jealous,
and smothers
that which might happen
if you opened your heart.

Open your mind,
let flow the art.
Exchange of ideas
is the place to start.

"Free your mind
and your ass will follow,"
close your mind
your life is hollow.

VINCIE

Was my young gay friend.
Very effeminate, very loving
we had a lot of fun
without the confusion
of sexuality.
Who knows really
what gay is
when you're 10 years old?

We had a secret society
"The Mannix Men."
We fashioned ourseles
as sleuths,
committed to finding truths.
We made up songs
and dance routines
harnessing the exuberance
of our youth.

Also, we were vandals.

His older brother
was a bully.
Slapped him around
called him sissy
and girl.

He was big and mean.
I was afraid of him.
He was the polar opposite
of sweet Vincie.
Vincie and I were friends.

There was only
the creativity
of our innocence.

Vincie died young.

Some years later
the older brother
shows up at my bar
on the south side of Chicago
on Christmas Eve.

I hadn't seen him in years,
we shared some beers.

Soon, he broke down.

"You were nice to my brother
he looked up to you. I wish I didn't do
what I did to him, but I didn't know,
and now I pay for it every day.
I wish I could take it all back."

But you can't.

This karmic comeuppance
is fully appropriate.

Let this be a reminder
to appreciate
those around you
even if you can't relate.

RIP Vince Santoro

A DARK LOVE SONG

The path is perilous
rocky, rutted, steep
bordered by forest
dense, dark, deep.
A simple misstep
could break one's neck
our climb to the clearing
Is an arduous trek.

No creatures are present
none impedes our pace;
we are plodding peasants
resolved to claim our place.
Yet storm clouds hover
dark forces assembling
we continue to elevate
despite the earth's trembling.

The powers that be
are hovering, growling
the dogs of war
are leashed, but howling;
if we don't reach the mesa
and the shit hits the fan
there will be no safety
for woman or man.

Still, we continue
our forward ascent
conscious of all
the trust that we've spent.

We've been sold out,
we've been misused,
but our will to survive
is not confused.

We have no need
for gods nor prophets,
nor golden idols
disguised as profits.
The markets will crash,
institutions will fall,
we'll keep on climbing
in spite of it all.

MORNING MADRIGAL

C'mon little darlin'
Let's get in off the street
Have a sip of somethin'
cook up somethin' to eat.

Then wrap ourselves
in each other
in a grip both strong and sweet
you can rub my belly
I'll rub your feet.

In this grip of earnest passion
while outside the world burns
we grasp with hope
avoiding the rope
give each other generous turns.

In these dark hours
of a destiny
we thought we'd never see,
the universe has coalesced
in the space between you and me.

The bitchy hyenas
of politics
and their greedy machinations
have no sway over us
in our positive vibrations.

You and I are all we have
in this mess of humanity.
If we hold each other close
and listen
we may salvage our sanity.

THE QUESTION

On the threshold
Of my imminent death
At the cliff's edge
Prior to my leap,
I question what
In this life
I have to keep.

My energy
And passion
Has been disbursed
I have been immersed
In other's drama
And trauma
Not the least of which
Was the madness
Of my mama.

Now seeking
To penetrate
The veil
Of the "afterlife"
Without a knife
And plunge into
The unknown
Chewing into
This mortal bone
I feel it's time
To go it alone.

I stand naked
Not afraid
A gentle breeze
Urges me forward
Into the abyss
Of bliss
The kiss of death
I take a breath.

Naaaah, I think.
There is wine to drink,
And friends
With glasses to clink,
And music music music,
And girls to squeeze
And love
Books to read
Stories to tell
Idiot ideas to quell,
So before I send
Myself to potential hell

I've got work to do.

The reaper must wait
'til a later date.
While with a grim smile
I pursue my fate.

MORNING BIRDS

Reality has been upended
truth has been suspended
common sense has ended
these rifts will not be mended.

PT Barnum
could not have foreseen while
spinning in his grave
a sketch this obscene.

Groucho
is amused, but pissed
in his wildest dreams
could not imagine this.

Shakespeare is chuckling,
shaking his head
glad this happened
centuries after he's dead.

Curly, Larry, Moe
would know just what to do;
poke all of our eyes out
and murdalize us too.

Abraham Lincoln
is stroking his beard
wondering how
it got this weird

Mark Twain
whose river has been roiled
America, he thinks
is a good walk spoiled.

Amelia Earhart
despite her errant flight
wants to come back
and make things right.

Marie Sklodowska Curie
working in her lab
wonders if there's something
of value left to grab.

Vince Lombardi
Clenches his fists
imagines a game plan
to get us out of this.

Martin Luther King
gazing out from his steeple
sheds a lone tear
"My people, my people".

"But you and I,
we've been through this
and this is not our fate;
let us not talk falsely now
the hour's getting late."

SELF DEFINITION

I know, I know
I'm some kind of junkie.
I stay up all night
drinking
getting funky.

Sometimes
I smoke a little weed
searching for what I need
to put my frantic mind to sleep,
yet hoping to keep
those maybe good ideas
in the forefront,
secondary
to the motherlode
of responsibility
that has me on the road
to humanity,
on the edge
of more or less sanity.

Amidst my hopes
for peace and serenity
myriad ideas present to me
snow globes of possibility;
shake 'em up and see
what might be
eventually,
with the everpresent
possibility
of civility
in our society.
After the upheaval
the flurried fragments

may settle,
into place,
with the will of a God
and the forces that be
into a globe of fine fettle.

Every
stupid little beat
of my gullible heart
refutes the cruelty
of the crude art
of financial,
classist, racist
manipulation
of our population
the desecration
of the pride of our nation.

We must regain
our constitution;
seeking not restitution
for the myriad sins
of our history.
Rather,
let the blood of life
flow through us
into us
creating connection
through the axons
of our experience
resolving mystery
bringing us hence
to a place
where a handshake
or a warm embrace
actually means something.

THE HUG

I seek perfection
in the expression
of my soul
if I actually have one.

I seek to love
powerfully
perpetually
honestly.

I seek to rend
the layers
of my being
like those multiple
candy wrappers
you must unravel
to get to the sweets.

I seek to bleed
the violence of my being
the violence I am seeing
the violence of emotion
that is freeing
for the fragile crisp
of humanity
that inhabits me.

I am a dangerous man.
I ask questions.
I do things.
I look you in the eye.

I hug you
like my life depends upon it
because it does.

SWEEPING

This morning
I am weeping
instead of sleeping.

I ain't weeping
'cause I'm a pussy,
I'm weeping
for our fate.

Observing the state
of our humanity
the overflowing
insanity
makes me blue
because I care
about you
and me
and everybody
Everywhere.

Except for assholes.
They seem to be
cropping up
Exponentially.

What the hell
happened to
Empathy?

Are we so
self-absorbed
and dense
that we've lost
our common sense?

When we lift
each other
we lift ourselves.

We claim
to be a culture
modeled
after a cat
named
Jesus Christ.

I see His name
everywhere
but not his presence.

I want Him back.

PARADE

Welcome to madness
the "go to" destination
of those who give up
out of frustration.

Unable
unwilling
to accept
anything
but top billing
elbows on
the windowsill
watching
the world pass
another ball drops
as you sit on your ass.

Digging deep
into
the barren mine
of self-pity
seeking rootstock
of enmity
vicious tendrils
of inability
comes a weed
borne
of poisonous
need.

Pretty petals
adorn this flower
masquerading

its subtle power
of infection
of spirit.
Put it in
your lapel
wear it
announce to all
your inverse
merit.
Pride
is chain mail
for inherent
weakness
a parasol
of falsity
embroidered
with bleakness.

Strip tease
with your finery
of failure
whatever
good you've got
cannot be clothed;
cast off the madness
or forever
be loathed.

I cannot tell
further lies,
this dirge
identifies
all the madness
before my eyes.

I REMEMBER PETE MONACO

He was the coach
of the McGuane Steelers,
the park district football team
with whom I got my ass kicked
as a teen.

He was a short
slump-shouldered
potbellied
balding old Dago
with curly white hair
falling around his ears.

He owned a junkyard
drove a '54 Ford pickup
welded pipes around the bed
which we held onto
as we sped
to the not so distant parks
to do battle
with the others of our ilk
of different colors
and zip codes.

"Don't be afraid of the Black boys," he said.
"They bleed like ya
they hurt like ya
they stink like ya."

He taught
fundamentals.
How to block and tackle
How to hold the ball
to not fumble
as you tried to run
for a first down
through the hole
created by your lineman.

Mostly how not to fear.

He told us
how lucky we were
to have helmets
shoulder pads
equipment.

How, as a kid
in the '40s
at Tilden High
he had to stuff his jersey
with straw
because there were no
shoulder pads.

How every game ended
with blood and respect
and echoing pain.

He tried to convey
in his antiquated way
how to be a man.

Now
many years later
as I try to be a man
in a different world

I remember Pete Monaco
with gratitude.

I am still blocking, tackling, running.

SUNRISE

Tumbling
out of the darkness
I chug down to the pier

Sun rising
easily in the east
enveloping me
in the glow
of no fear

I watch the ocean's
undulations;
the power
the glory
the force
that shapes nations.

I watch the surfers
poised
to catch a swell.
I am envious
I wish them well.

A mile offshore
the whales play.
They breach,
they spout
they greet the day.

I have the urge
to leap

into
the tidal surge
as if the water
would my soul
purge.

I stand pat;
no leaping
this morn
sip my coffee
blissful
that I have
been born
into this world
of natural beauty

In the midst
of the madness
of man's
machinations
I am ecstatic
in my current
destination.

The few
that crave power
fueled by greed
are missing
the substance;
their souls
cannot feed
upon the pageantry
of nature.

Their weakness
exacerbates
their need.

I'm happy
to be who I am
where I stand.
I cannot
stem the tide
of those
igniting
negative motion

only the ocean can.

Let us be the ocean.

AWAKEN

Pale light seeps through the shades
prior to the arrival of dawn.
The imminent day beckons
as the previous day yawns.

In what space of our minds
do we realize what we do?
Are yesterday, and the days before
the lack of action that we rue?

This day, on the doorstep,
knocking at our door
asking if we're satisfied
or if we want some more
of the shit we've heaped
upon ourselves
down on this killing floor?

Killing seems to be
that which we do best;
we've not yet been killed ourselves
(not yet)
but what about the rest?

When do we claim our humanness?
When do we refute our hate?
When do we take action
to avoid this toxic fate?

With open minds
and open arms
and a grateful open heart
we can dismantle
this pestilence
that threatens to tear us apart.

BACK OF THE BUS

This is what I know to be true.
If you love me, I may love you.
Love however, is not possession;
it can be an obsession.

It is mostly a shared mess.

We try to find ourselves
as we undress each other.
We think we'll find truth
under the covers.
We think we'll find truth
in the conversation of our bodies.

We'll walk away
sticky and sweet
with that moist memory
and anticipation of
when again we'll meet.

There's a little piece of me
that goes into you;
there's that drapery
of your body onto mine;
we are complicit
in this pleasure
it feels fine.

What have we accomplished?
Have we become one?
When we've drained each other?
Are we done?

I believe that actually
it's an exchange of thought.
An exchange of feeling
it's what we bought
in the markets of our lives.

We will continue.
We will repeat.
If we respect each other
we will keep our seat
on the back of this bus.

SOCIAL DISTANCE RESISTANCE

In my ignorant mind
"social" is something
we left behind
the discarded rind
of the beautiful fruit
that binds us together.

"Social" is what we do
and say
with each other
to keep the fear away.

"Social" is connection
communication
the oft unspoken hug
at the station
as we go our separate ways
with the anticipation
that we will meet again.

"Social" is the interaction
which gives us traction
on the slippery slope
of modern reality,
keeping us grounded
In the unbounded
miasma of banality.

"Social" is the balm
of emotion
and thought

the exchange
of energy
creating synergy
which keeps you part of me
particularly
when life conspires
to dispense
with our unity.

"Social"
to the charlatans
is unforgivable,
yet makes life liveable
for fools like me.

"Social"
is sharing ideas
while we undress
the garments of stress
and caress
each other's minds
leaving the falsehood
of dogma behind.

"Social" is what
I cannot live without,
despite my occasional need
for privacy.
It is liberty.

IMAGERY

I have written recently
of fights,
but I have witnessed
powerful sights;
the Grand Canyon at sunrise,
sunset, and midnights.

The powerful
sometimes placid
waters
of rivers, lakes, and streams
the sweet faces of mountains
upon which the sunlight gleams.

The golden or green
expanses of the plains
the huffing and puffing
of hard working trains.

The faces of beauties
the faces of the bereft
those whose fortunes
have mysteriously left.

The radiant glamour
of the ostentatious
big cities
selling sex, booze, drugs,
and somebody's titties.

Smashed faces
smashed cars
smashed idiots
in bars.

The underwater world
one must dive to see
the breathless energy
of those who long
to be free.

The leather bound books
The art in museums
The details on facades
if you look close enough
to see 'em.

The image, however,
that makes me whole
is when I perceive
the beauty
in another's soul.

SATELLITES

Watching the satellites
carve arcs
in the sky at night
reminds me that
we are miniscule
earthbound vessels
simple tools
pursuing our own capsules
of self indulgence.

The idea that
those orbiting cameras
might be interested
in what we do
is preposterous.
What we really need
is more angels
to foster us
through our ignorance
into a brighter light.

We live our lives
in our personal beat;
we work, we laugh,
we drink, we eat
sometimes that
which is not digestible.

Life is not
always the festival
we've hoped it would be
Particularly
in the overpopulated
madness
of our communities.

Overpopulated
Overregulated
Over fed
Over sedated
Over charged for everything
Over and over
validating the talking heads.

We must listen
to the voice within
the soaring aria
beneath the skin
the rapture
of the music
that comes out of the mind.

We must listen
listen listen
leaving the noise behind.

FERMENTATION

As I fester here
in my early morning
idiocy,
entertaining
preposterous ideas
it occurs to me:
why can't I be
who I want to be?

What do you do
to define you?

I've earned
what I've got
which ain't a lot
I've paid to play
I back up what I say
I've got blood on my hands
stains on my soul
yet through it all
I still feel whole.

I spit out words
searching for meaning;
if you're paying attention
I hope you're gleaning
something
from my experience.

Stick your icepick
into my heart
watch the blood flow
a flood
of passion
and mostly
good intention.

I can't punch hard enough
to break down the walls
of our obstinacy
yet perhaps you'll grasp
my hand and walk with me
into something like
spiritual intimacy.

We'll walk softly
with kindness
and peace.

We're here for a short time
with a limited lease.

RENT

Sometimes
before I fall asleep
I want to plunge
into the deep
dark night of eternity.

I do not want to wake
but rather
to slake my thirst
with the great unknown.

I feel myself
floating
in the amniotic fluid
of rebirth
removed from earth
steeped in the girth
of the past life's banality
the idiotic reality
of acquisitions
obtuse positions
of trying
to gain gain gain
again and again.

This peaceful
fetus floating
sailboating
into the cosmos
of possibility

impresses the fragility
of what we have
and have not.

Fortunately
I have a nice tack
and wind at my back
and no lack
of inspiration.
I can easily
transport myself
into the worlds
of past, present, future
without tensing
too intensely.

I feel the richness
of life
and all of its
vicissitudes
that do not denude
my attitude
or hunger
for experience.

I have paid my rents.

There will be more due
and I hope to
be equal or better to
these lifeline deadlines.
It's all one can do.

IN THE CRADLE

Once again
consumed by the night sky
the cosmos' twinkling eye
percussion provided by
crashing waves.
The tide is high.

The tide is high
in my spirit
though troubled
it may be.
In the dark of night
what matters
is what I hear
not what I see.

Constellations
a backdrop
for what I sense
what I feel;
conversations
with the universe
comfort me
keep it surreal.

I have no fear
of worldly powers
or their self serving design.
I take no rest
do my best
to keep my planet
in the proper trine.

We must extend
our hands to each other
in this tumultuous
cosmic stew.
Let us see, hear, feel
the truth of what's real
we'll see this crisis through.

ONE WAY TICKET

I'm happy to be
a ne'er do well
with a one way ticket
to a version of hell.

I'm happy to be
a stranger
in a world
of feigned familiarity.
I'll play the clown
as I go down
in a blaze
of ironic hilarity.

I'm happy
to tromp through society
with boots
not of propriety
but of broad variety
fashioned with soles
resistant to the coals
of fake piety.

I'm happy
to have joy
in my humble existence,
driven forward
not with wisdom
but with mindful persistence.

I'm happy
to express
without duress
those things
that make me human,
knowing full well
on this road to hell
you'll remember me
as a true man.

I'm happy
with every breath I take
aware that my time is brief
understanding
that in this tree of life
I've been a somewhat
useful leaf.

A LEARNING CURVE

The first time that she caught my eye,
I was hungry, and determined to try
To possess her body, and her soul;
I was on the hunt, I was not whole.

As time passed by, in my pursuit
I learned that all my points were moot.
I yearned to own what would never be mine,
I had lust and thirst, but no actual spine.

I had to beat back my shallow desire,
emerge from my egotistical mire,
recognize her humanity
or drown in my own vanity.

Like any thwarted predator,
my tack was to discredit her;
not in public, in my mind
I had to leave my pride behind.

After months steeped in futility
I was visited by humility;
forsaking my internal greed
I found a greater lust to feed.

I tripped upon a lust for truth
Eschewing the madness of my youth
Looking her straight in the eye
I thanked her for the lesson and said
goodbye.

What came to pass, eventually
Was a friendship that came naturally.
I was learning to be a real man,
Each day doing the best I can.

Beyond my greatest expectation,
I took a spiritual vacation
She saw the change I made in life
Took my hand, became my wife.

It's said that patience is a virtue
I have found this to be true;
If you're governed by your lust
Your lust becomes you.

MOONFUL FEVER

Full moon a blazing nipple
with a gauzy aureole
laughing at me
and all I might be
exposing my lupine soul

the ocean a sonic backdrop
seducing my wolfish mind
the steel cold night
the hypnotic light
leaving this world behind

I've been a walking receptacle
for the illness of the earth
the madness of men
in the lunar mayhem
since the moment of my birth

we suck the teat of technology
shit you can buy for some bucks
the toys, the noise
the girls and boys
lunatics run amok

"love you to the moon and back"
is a common expression
but if you knew
what the moon had for you
you'd schedule a therapy session

Luna has influence
Beyond our comprehension
Beyond tides and menses
beyond our senses
cruel mother of invention

Full moon beckons to me
a modern day Lon Chaney
turns me into a beast
lusting for a blood feast
a ritual to sustain me

I embrace my inner wolf
I howl with the moon
but I do no harm
and bear no arms whistle a wolf-moon tune

UNDEAD BLUES

In my little coffin-bed
Dracu-like, resting 'til sunset,
prospecting in my head
steeping in the soil
of my lifelong toil
seeping through keyholes
so as not to roil
the innocent sleeper.
Imbibing greedily
the life that has bled
I yearn for the slumber
that gives peace to the dead.

"What's on the other side of that
door?" we wonder.
In quest of that answer
through life we wander.
Wake up sleepers!
Do not squander
that which we've been given;
soon enough life will be driven
from us, snatched
from our tenuous grasp.
Poisoned by the cosmic asp
which governs all mortality.

We sleep, we awaken
constantly aching
for the hungry grip
of money, or fame
or love—it's all the same.

The hunger, the thirst
the dream bubbles that burst
urging us to the edge of the cliff
naked and shaking
peering into the abyss.

We do not leap,
We embrace our lives
and our loves
every moment that drove
us to this juncture.
We do not allow
desperation
to puncture
our fragile constitution.
we recover ourselves;
personal absolution
for our humanity,
giggling giddily
we resume our insanity.

Some days
it's all we've got;
better to have it
than not.
While our minds are active,
and our passions are hot,
we continue to move
our needles in the groove
in the name of love.

VISITATION

She comes to me
in the middle of the night
bathed in phosphorescent light.
I can't see her clearly
she emanates might
I am frozen, crippled
I can't take flight.

"Listen, young one
you're moving too fast.
You can't get to the next stage
'til you distance your past."

She speaks to me
like a long ago teacher;
I want to protest,
but I know I can't reach her.

She's here to give warning
perhaps to save my soul
but I can't slow down now
I'm on a hell of a roll.

She mutes her voice
to a mothering tone
"Slow down, slow down
you're not alone.
The people around you
are fully vested
in your success
are you interested

in seeing this voyage
to its natural end?
Or are you possessed
with what's around the next bend?"

The answer, I guess, is
I don't know.
I've never been a cat
that can move very slow.

Yet I heed her words
like an acolyte;
humbly taking wisdom
that gets me through the night.

In the morning
her glow
still permeates my mind;
I'm not sure what happened
but I'm hoping to find
the psychic detritus
that I need to leave behind
in order to follow
and eventually lead.

LOST AND FOUND

So much has been lost
An equal amount found
On rough seas we've been tossed
but landed on solid ground.

We've been disappointed,
misrepresented
responsible for all of that
to which we have consented.

Do not underestimate
the power of rampant greed;
the hungry bastards salivate
upon our virtue they feed.

The law of the jungle
Some say dog eat dog;
a simple justification
for the amoral smog.

Our hopeful spirituality
makes us think
that truth will win;
the devil winks and nods
cracks a knowing grin.

Yet we soldier on
undaunted by the lies;
get thee behind me Satan
children avert your eyes.

STORM

It is raining with purpose,
the deluge creating
myriad percussions.
No need for discussion,
just listen to the rain.

The thrumming, drumming
on my roof
enhanced by the drip
of the neighbor's gutter
the rain utters
that which we dare not say.

Here comes the thunder!
Tearing asunder
the peace of the rhythm;
a natural schism between
electric and water
A bitch-fest between
Poseidon and his daughter.

As a child, I was told
thunder was clouds
bumping into each other,
atmospheric smash of Sumos
sending the dogs
beneath the beds.

I miss the thunderstorms
of my midwestern youth.
Lightning blazing the sky
bright blue-white,
turning night into daylight.

Caterwauling winds
collapsing powerlines
felling trees
blowing off the weaker doors
torrents of water
tormenting housewives
who scurry to shut the windows
frantically pulling
the laundry off the lines.

I imagined the storms
as giants hurling
boulders at each other,
titans engaged in battle
as Zeus guffawed mortals cowering
beneath the power
of the natural world.
I was afraid.

As I aged,
I learned awe and respect for
the atmospheric energy
that I saw.
I learned
to get naked in the rain,
clothes simply an encumbrance
separating us
from nature's stain.

I long to feel
that innocence again.

I ONCE WAS THE WOLFMAN, JACK

The little fat, ripe full moon
is glowering at me.

"Wolfman" she says
"Why are you sitting around
relaxing
when you should be out
ravaging and savaging?"

"Sweetie" I reply,
"I am 322 years old.
That shit doesn't come
easy anymore."

The days of
"You better stay away
from him, he'll rip your
lungs out Jim"
are long gone.

I like a nice smooth whiskey
and a good cigar.
I don't have to prowl
or go too far
to satisfy my bloodlust.

I can still get it
if I really need it
but there's only so much
flesh rending
that'll make your weekend
that much better.

Now I sit in my armchair
in my Pendleton sweater,
recalling the glory days,
the gory days
when all the flatfoots
came hunting for me
after I had ravaged
savaged
shredded into
human cabbage
those innocents
lost enough
to meet me on the Moors.

I'm tired of smashing
through doors
shattering glass
evading silver bullets.

I still have a few tricks left
if out of my hat
I can pull it.

Now I let my kids
do the heavy lifting.

Mostly they're not
ripping souls asunder
they're just grifting.

Yes, they all work
For the government.

INFECTION

I am an infection
Creating connection
Across the synapse
Between your being
And wanting to be.
Asking wordlessly
Will you dance with me?

I am a no-account
Not invested
In your bank account
Not wanting to mount you
But rather to prick
Your nascent fount
Passion
See where you flow
Wanting to know
Where you will
Allow yourself to go.

Your uncommon sense
Orders you refuse me
Denying you the right
To use me
To take you to that place
The mesa of the muse
A joyous cruise
Beyond the limits
Of the safety
That you choose.

My lure is not so strong
To urge you along
To unstrip your bounds
Show you around
The world of unfelt sound;
"All you can do
is do what you must."

I have failed you.

FREEDOM

I'm not the sexual being
I used to be.
It's the synergy
of the meeting
that sets me free.

The entwining
of the heart and mind
helps me
leave the world behind.

The body craves
the sweet soft flesh;
the spirit beckons
to another to mesh.

My erect appendage
the flagpole of manhood
is secondary
to the urge to do good.

Wholeness now
is what I seek;
my lust is not unique.
The brilliant corners
define my quest:
find the beauty, the truth,
extinguish the rest.

The lust, the greed,
the driving forces of our need,
have planted
an amoral seed.

Now
our better selves recover
tell the venal ones
to move over.

This is an admission of guilt.
My willfulness will not wilt;
we will not waste the house we built.

Responsibility
and its gravitational pull
persuades me that
we will, we will
endure, prosper, love
until...

DIVING IN

I have leapt
from the precipitous
cliff's edge
into the deepest
fathoms of sleep.

I have pierced
the surface
of consciousness
into the limitless
depths of possibility.

Wading around
in the blindness
of opportunity,
I hold my breath
and things happen to me.

Frequently I fight
demons of the past
wrestling with anxiety
the meanness of society.

Sometimes I fly.
These are the good nights
when, with eagle eyes
I can spy
what beckons for change.

I communicate
with lost loved ones,
tango with future friends,
lust after the unattainable—
with passion that never ends.

I am pursued
by hostile forces,
my feet seemingly
bound in lead.
The bastards never catch me
I awaken instead.

I've caught myself
giggling
drooling
shaking
my nocturnal
existence
might leave me aching
for more.

If I could leave
this body behind
shuck the bonds
of perceived reality
diving into my dreams
leaving behind life's banality
I would never hear the screams
of those trapped
in a world
with no imagination.

FATHER'S DAY

I see my old man
when I look in the mirror;
enigmatic in life
post-mortem clearer and clearer.

He spent much of his life
behind the wheel of a truck;
slumped forward, sweaty
muscling through urban muck.

Beefy up top
Flat-topped high and tight,
a working class hero
ever ready for a fight.

He had a crude sense of humor
dished out dirty ditties
gun slinging limericks
full of asses and titties.

He taught me to cuss
taught me to brawl,
he was a sweetheart, a softie
in spite of it all.

Saddled with a family
he had not expected,
he was nonetheless
properly directed.

There was food on the table
private education
we were clothed and happy
but knew not a vacation.

He was married four times
tried to get it right
needing a woman
to get through the night.

In the later chapters
with nothing to lose,
he marinated himself
in cigarettes and booze.

The reaper came one night
saying "Enough is enough!"
punctured his heart
the end of Pa Puff.

These verses do not
tell the whole tale;
he was a man in America
yet he was never for sale.

FATE OF FIDO

I left my life last night.
Slipped out of my body
into the light.
The light was water
an eternal sea.
It saw me coming.
It was waiting for me.

I dove in deep
and swam around
there was a recognizable sound
barking dogs
in a sub-aquatic pound.

They were waiting
for someone to free them.
I would if I could see them.

The density of the water
partially blinded me
but I could hear
their yips and yaps
impassioned howls
some with foam
dripping from their jowls
waiting for a rescue
that wouldn't come from me.

We are all barking dogs
wanting to be fed
and petted
scratched behind the ears;
to be held and loved
until the end of our years.

We'll be loyal.
We'll be true.
But at some point
we're still gonna
shit on the rug.

I was lucky.
I emerged.
Came back into
my body after being
submerged
in a metaphor.

I woke up smiling
with dog breath,
happy to not have
dreamt my death.
Wondering
What we do this for.

ELECTION DAY

Funny thing
about an election,
swap out a letter
you've got a stiffy.
That makes the election
somewhat iffy.
You know how that works…
lots of blood in a member
but then flaccid
after a day in November.
The problem is
it's a short term contest
for a long term gain;
leaves most citizens
in a state of pain.
How do we fix
what does not create us?
which, more or less
can asphyxiate us?
The answer, now,
is nothing.
We've ordained our fate;
we've kowtowed
to accusations
paranoia, and hate.

It's like
a disappointing
first date;
you end up
with a loser
found out too late.
Yet you're still
stuck with the check,
coughing up Drachmas
and listening to dreck.
At the end of the day
you recognize
the wreck
of what we have become:
soulless, divided
driven by bad behavior
ostensibly guided
by a nonexistent savior.

At least we voted for it.

ANOTHER TUESDAY BLUESDAY

I got the blues so deep
20,000 leagues
under the deep blue sea.
Blues so deep
they asphyxiate me.

They like to make me weep.
They like to make me fight;
torture my sorry ass,
make me stay up all night.

Worryin' 'bout my people
Worryin' 'bout my life.
Seems all we got these days
is heartache and strife.

I look for silver linings
I find them time to time;
I go into my little blue room,
bang out a little rhythm and rhyme.

The guiding force of love
has been battered and bruised;
our better passions and intentions
have been woefully misused.

BB King asked
"How Blue Can You Get?"
Well I've spoken to the oracle
And she said we ain't there yet.

More hard roads to travel,
more blues to bank;
the blues is up to my eyes now,
I can see how deep we've sank.

Well, I pray, and I ain't a prayin' man,
but I pray and pray and pray,
that at the end of this dark tunnel
we'll see the blue sky of a new day.

DIRTY JOKE

There is a little place
inside
that keeps us whole.
Slaps us in the face
when we try to erase
that which comprises
our soul.

Soul you see
is singular.
We are the atoms
of soul composition.
When we compromise
falsely advertise
succumb to superstition,
we mortgage ourselves
to a lower power
a subordinate position.

When we elevate
ourselves
and our earthmates
we bolster our opposition
to that which
denigrates us
urging us toward
Perdition.

If we acted upon
what we purport to believe
not self deceive
we might support
each other and relieve
the biases
we wear on our sleeve.

Hahahahahahaha!
Just kidding!
We're screwed.

SOUTHERN PACIFIC

She rides me
like a freight train
chugging down the track
legs around my torso
talons in my back.

Teeth in my neck
sucking my warm blood
smashing through
the dam wall
bracin' for the flood.

Smokestack lightnin'
blowin' out the blues
not a care in the world
burnin' up the fuse.

First a breathy whimper
then some earnest moans
cashing in years
of unpaid loans.

Just a couple of teens
makin' up for lost time
no moss on these stones
but mud on these boots
scrapping through the climb
that returns us to our roots.

Every stoned idea
I've ever thought or said
is manifested in the madness
that happens in this bed.

After this train ride
I sleep another hour
then enter the world of men
where I manifest my power,
praying to whatever god
to not let this milk sour.

CLEOPATRA OF MY DREAMS

In the voluptuous encounter
(Take her home and mount her!)
I found a new friend
whom will live with me
to the infernal end.

In my prospecting
for sensual gold,
aromas and textures
both subtle and bold
enraptured my senses;
my feelings unrolled.

Some truth was revealed
in the nest where we nestled,
a bridge was erected
on the mat where we wrestled.

It's not what you think,
it's not about sex.
It's about commonality
and emotional treks.
In the communion of mind
as we gripped our behinds
something other occurred
outside of the lines.
In the admission
of our mutual need
an idea took root
a fine fertile seed.

We talked and laughed
Through the dark cashmere night,
professing our weakness
and lack of keen sight.
While we burned up our jones
with the fire of our youth,
we met on the plane
of our innocent truth.

She left before dawn
while I slept like the dead
her parting expression
a soft kiss on my head.

I must confess
in my mind somewhat twisted
she was my fantasy girl;
she never existed.

BLESS ME FATHER

My past is coming to get me,
seeking retribution
for all that I did
when I was a kid.

Which, for practical purposes
could be any day before today.
I can't believe I lived that way.

Trying to shed my kindness
and molt into a man
my retrospection, self inspection
lays bets that I can.

Those black boys
we fought and beat
in the rancid heat
of the south side
do not haunt me,
yet I remember.

My knuckles
reverberated
from the shock of fist on skull
then, with the left,
the lips we perforated.
Later, many times,
I was karmically
compensated.

Three dark men
randomly directed
pummeled me
like kids at a party

punching that blowup clown doll
with sand in the base;
I weebled, I wobbled,
but did not fall on my face;
I held my place,
however debased.

Now,
trying to be a man
having no desire
to engage in combat
with my fellow humans
of any race, color, gender, creed
I seek to do the proper deed.

In my molting into manhood
seeking always to do well
as opposed to petty evil
keeping it on the level
doing what I should.

A call to action here and now
for those who want to grow;
eschew the bias and the violence,
mine that which your soul should know;
the proper path of love and kindness
the righteous way to go.

A cautionary note:
mistake not my kindness for weakness.
Snowflakes do not melt
but meld with others
creating an avalanche.

A SUNDAY LAMENTATION

Everything is tainted.
Everything is stained.
Everyone is wounded.
Everyone is pained.

You can hear the moaning groaning
from the ravaged masses.
You can hear the porcine grunting
from the fearful well-armed asses.

You can feel the silent howling
from the school's empty rooms.
You can feel the trepidation
from the babies in the wombs.

We are slapped with impunity
by the greed-mongers in power.
We are slapped in our community
not allowed to flower.

Those of you who believe in God
are gifted with hope and joy.
Those of you who don't believe
have no godhead to employ.

The anger is accumulating
as well as the frustration.
The people that dare to speak out
denied peaceful demonstration.

In the pursuit of happiness
we have been misdirected.
In the pursuit of happiness
we've not gotten what we expected.

We still have, for the moment,
the peace and solace of the earth.
We still have, for the moment,
Nature's purity and worth.

We must flush from our porcelain porticos
those that wield the banner of greed
We must flush in embarrassment
the corruption that we feed.

We must act in solidarity,
we must embrace each other.
We must act with vision and clarity
we've got one world, no other.

A RIVER

Sitting on a log
on the river bank
the log an extension
of myself.
A gnarly old appendage
of a used to be tree.
No longer attached to the mother trunk
disconnected from roots
steeped in my own funk
seeking not reconnection
but individual expression:
once a limb of a sturdy tree
now just driftwood
a branch called me.

The river is violent.
Fueled by the runoff
of generations
of malcontent;
not a benign
trickle down,
but a torrent
in which many
will drown.

The water is murky
angry and dark.
Where once
I angled for rainbows
in the eddies and pools

now piranhas thrive
hungry for the flesh
and blood of fools.

I long for the rivers
of my youth,
cool water healing me
fending off summer's
heat, humidity
clear enough to see
the riverbed,
current urging me
toward what lay ahead.
Relax, accept the flow,
unafraid of where I might go;
the river was infinity.

Perhaps I'll jump in the river
try to go with the flow
shoot the rapids,
avoid the rocks
to a future I don't know.
I can't control the river
nor regain my youth;
things will never be
what they once were.
The river is the truth.

WHAT HAPPENS WHILE I SLEEP

In the middle of the night
as I lay in the dark
my spirit departs me
to take a stroll in the park.

Does a soft shoe by the fountain
carves my name in a tree
does a two-step up a mountain
laughing giddily.

Gives the finger to the devil,
dirty limericks with the saints,
finds a morose Van Gogh,
sits beside him and paints.

Meets a gaggle of virgins
dancing 'round a maypole
whispers sweet nothings,
leaves them pure and whole.

Meets a hustler on a soapbox
shilling pie in the sky;
he's an elected official,
can't figure out why.

The sun is now rising,
it's time to go home;
my spirit re-enters
and brings me this poem.

A FICTION

The virus got me.
It set me free
from the bonds
of humanity.

I'm floating now,
like a hawk in the wind
all my worries
left behind.

Lofting about
I can see
my friends and family
they're doing just fine
some of them even miss me.

I have no hunger
no fear
no longing
for what I once held dear.

There is no "weather,"
it's all the same season.
My penis no longer
governs my reason.

Most of what I observe
is what I thought
the actions I embraced
those that I fought.

This other life,
eternity
appeals to me:
No expectations
No excuses
No apologies
No competition
No rules
No nine to five
No schools
No traffic
No fines
No waiting in lines.

Eventually,
there will be
things that I miss.
A chat with a friend,
an affectionate kiss,
a glass of good wine,
a home cooked meal
the ability to
articulate what I feel
to someone who
actually gets it.

The beauty
of our natural world
which for many years
made love to my senses
mountains, beaches,

fields without fences
wildflower perfume
briny ocean air
the small of the old lady's
cooking downstairs,
music

Many things to long for—
perhaps I missed the boat
but now I've got a nice tailwind
so I'll just smile and float.

A BRIEF PRAYER FROM A GODLESS MAN

In this time of crisis,
I'm feeling quite ecstatic!
My soul is in the basement
my heart is holed up in the attic.
My brain is somewhere in between
trying to sift through all the static;
what used to be reality
is unpredictable, erratic.

The source of my inexplicable bliss
is a mystery to me;
but I know that when we break through
this wall of idiocy
we'll come to better understand
how it feels to be free.

We're searching for something to blame,
like it's a plague we don't deserve,
when the wheels of life start rolling again
we'll have to determine who to serve.

Some of us claim to be masters,
some prefer to be slaves,
but the choices we make here and now
will follow us to our graves.

So "cowboy up!" now kiddies,
and put away your guns,
we think we're singled out in this,
but we're not the only ones.

It's called a "global pandemic"
and it's rampant world wide,
Our cures must be systemic,
if we are to stem the tide.

There is a void in leadership
but there are some rays of light
so hug your loved ones, and yourselves
and don't give up the fight.

Whatever entity you worship
I hope it's benevolent
because the last thing we need now
is a spirit that's malevolent.

I sit here now in my darkened room
pecking at the keys
sending out love to everyone
I implore you do the same please!

YES, I LOVE YOU.
SEE YOU IN THE NEXT

Sucked into
a vortex of fate
I've got no time to hate;
stuff to do
I can't be late.

Like the old
George Reeves Superman
I'm out the window
into the black & white sky
no time to wonder
where I'm going
or why.

I pause to ask
but there is no substance
in my knowing;
Life's current,
unrepentant,
keeps flowing.

Bulletproof
I descend
into the morass
of humans
their stain
the rash of man
grips me
like the
impervious net
trapping
missile-fish
into a 6 oz. can.

I bellow into
the indifferent void
attempting
to advocate
for myself
and peers
received by
silent jeers
from the
power mongers
buffered
by their greed
their fears.

Delayed
by the saltwater apathy
of the necktied
naysayers,
nonetheless
uttering prayers
for losers like me
denied
eternally.

Yet we persist
in the silent
death march
of all who are born
into this mess.

We undress,
expose ourselves
to the naked truth
of our reality
resolute
confident
in the possibilities
beyond our
fatality.